To:

_____

From:

_____

Date:

_____

a collection of stories,
quotes, scriptures,
and inspirational thoughts

a Touch

of love to say thank you

HOWARD
PUBLISHING CO.

A Touch of Love to Say Thank You © 2002 Howard Publishing Company
All rights reserved. Printed in Mexico

Published by Howard Publishing Co., Inc.,
3117 North 7th Street, West Monroe, LA 71291-2227

Contributors: Gary Myers, Debbie Webb, Mary Hollingsworth

Special thanks to Susan Duke for permission to use her story "In the Arms of an Angel."

02 03 04 05 06 07 08 09 10 11   10 9 8 7 6 5 4 3 2 1

Edited by Philis Boultinghouse
Concept and design by Steve Diggs and Friends, Nashville

ISBN: 1-58229-229-9

Unless otherwise noted, Scripture quotations are taken from the Holy Bible, New International Version, Copyright © 1973, 1978, 1984 International Bible Society. Used by permission of Zondervan Bible Publishers. Scripture quotations marked NLT are taken from the Holy Bible, New Living Translation, copyright © 1996. Used by permission of Tyndale House Publishers, Inc., Wheaton, Illinois 60189. All rights reserved.

Our purpose at Howard Publishing is to:
- *Increase faith* in the hearts of growing Christians
- *Inspire holiness* in the lives of believers
- *Instill hope* in the hearts of struggling people everywhere

Because He's coming again!

A Touch of Love to Say
Thank You

Thankful
Heartfelt
Awesome
Natural
Kindness
You-nique
Optimistic
Unforgettable

CHAPTER 1

Thankful

If there's one word that goes unsaid too many times, it's *thanks*. This little book is my way of saying, "I'm thankful for you!"

I'm thankful for

* your friendship
* your love
* your caring nature
* your sense of humor
* your being there

Your life has touched mine in so many ways. Thanks for all that you do. Most of all, thanks for just being you.

PHILIPPIANS 1:3

"I thank my God

every time

I remember you."

3

No duty is more urgent

than that of returning thanks.

—Saint Ambrose

4

In the Arms of an Angel

When the phone rang and I heard my friend Charlet's tearful voice, I knew something was wrong. Her daughter-in-law had just miscarried the baby that would have been Charlet's first grandchild. For five months she'd excitedly anticipated the birth of this precious new life.

Charlet was heartbroken. However, as a pastor's wife, she knew she'd have to be strong and attend to responsibilities for the following day's church service.

I couldn't get Charlet's grieving voice out of my mind. While loading breakfast dishes into the dishwasher, I tried to think of a special gift that would offer my friend some small comfort and expression of compassion. I thumbed through my mind's index of ideas, but nothing seemed right. As I cleaned my blue tile countertop with my dishtowel, I wiped around a little clay figurine of a chubby-faced angel holding a baby in its arms.

Chapter One: *Thankful*

This little angel had special meaning to me. I keep it in my kitchen, where I spend many hours, away from the angel collection displayed in my living room. My husband, Harvey, gave me this angel on the first Mother's Day after we lost our son, Thomas.

I remembered that each time Charlet had visited my home, she had admired the angel and its significance. I normally don't like shopping on Saturdays, but I put down my dishtowel, grabbed my purse, and went to a specialty shop to find the exact angel. Later that afternoon, my mission was accomplished. The next morning, Harvey and I decided we'd attend Charlet's church rather than our own.

We eased into the back row as the worship service began. After the first song, Pastor Ken initiated a time of greeting one another. When Charlet turned and saw me walking toward her, a well of tears filled her eyes. I handed her the gift and said, "Why don't you open this now? I have a feeling you need what's in here today." As she opened the gift, her face emanated a heavenly glow.

"Suzie, you couldn't have known this, but just after I found out we'd lost baby Katherine, I closed my eyes and envisioned an angel holding her. Then immediately I remembered the little angel in your kitchen. I thanked God for showing me she was safely carried to heaven in the arms of an angel."

How can we thank God enough for you

in return for all the joy we have

in the presence of our God

because of you?

1 Thessalonians 3:9

8

But friendship is precious,

not only in the shade,

but in the sunshine of life;

and thanks to a benevolent arrangement of things,

the greater part of life is sunshine.

—Thomas Jefferson

Thankful

Heartfelt

Awesome

Natural

Kindness

You-nique

Optimistic

Unforgettable

CHAPTER 2

Heartfelt

Have you ever heard someone say, "That touched my heart-strings"? Whoever coined the phrase must have known something about music. In some strange way, kind deeds and words of love tune the heart the way a musician's hands tune an instrument to perfection.

Strings that have been stretched too taut grow brittle with time, as the heart without kindness atrophies and becomes a heart of stone. Strings that are never used grow dull and lifeless, as a loveless life feels useless and meaningless. But the right tension of love and kindness keeps the heart tuned at peak performance. Out of that heart, music flows freely.

Thank you for touching my heart.

PSALM 16:9, 11

Therefore my heart is glad and

my tongue rejoices.…

You have made known to me

the path of life;

you will fill me with joy in your

presence, with eternal pleasures

at your right hand.

The happiness of life

is made up of minute fractions—

the little, soon forgotten charities of a kiss or smile,

a kind look, a heartfelt compliment,

and the countless infinitesimals of pleasurable

and genial feeling.

—Samuel Taylor
Coleridge

Tattered and Loved

It was a beautiful, crisp fall evening in October, and the sky was ablaze with the last bronze blast from the sun's descent just above the thin line of the Tuscaloosa horizon. Tom and Hannah had decided to celebrate, along with their one-year-old daughter, Rachel. Tom had been promoted at the automobile plant where he was employed, and an increase in pay was a welcome reprieve. Things had been tight with the new baby and the new house, and this unexpected blessing was going to remove a great deal of strain.

They had chosen their favorite family restaurant as the location to commemorate this day of deliverance from the stresses of too many bills and too little money. The fireplace in the center of the room danced with light, and the warmth was a delicious contrast to the coolness that was settling in with the setting sun. They nestled together in a booth near the hearth, and the young couple began a playful discussion about what they would splurge on for their

Chapter Two: *Heartfelt*

evening meal. Evelyn, a waitress who had been their favorite since they started coming here five years ago, took their order and shared in their good news. The evening simply couldn't have been going any better.

Midway through the meal, a stranger appeared at the counter. He was dressed shabbily from head to toe. The black coat that covered his filthy overalls looked as though it had been cut into shreds around the hemline that hung to his knees. A foul odor indicated too many days without a bath and too many nights in the streets. His hair hung in oily strands down to his shoulders and looked as though it had not been brushed in ages. The appendages that appeared from his gray fingerless gloves looked greasy, and dirt lined his fingernails. There was little expression on his face, and no one bothered to say anything to him. He simply ordered a cup of coffee in a gruff voice and looked about the restaurant until it came.

Tom and Hannah were both lost in the festive spirit of the evening, so neither of them even noticed the lone stranger—at least at first. Amidst their hearty laughter, Hannah heard a squeal of joy from Rachel's lips. As she turned, she saw the filthy man smiling at Rachel. He was playing peekaboo, placing his weathered hands over his eyes and then dropping them suddenly. His toothless grin nauseated Hannah, but tiny Rachel was overjoyed with her newfound friend. Her bright blue eyes grew bigger with each attempt on the part of the stranger to thrill her. She began to rock back and forth in her high chair and laugh with unrestrained enthusiasm.

Hannah was growing quite uncomfortable with the interaction between her daughter and the strange man. She urged Tom to make the stranger stop. Tom looked at the two of them—what a contrast. They were lost in their delight in each other; so Tom told Hannah to relax.

The whole restaurant seemed to get involved in observing the activities of the tattered stranger at the counter and the fresh-faced little girl who found him absolutely irresistible. Some signaled disgust at the exchange between the two, but many found the interaction more entertaining than their own conversation.

Hannah encouraged Tom to pay the bill so they could escape this embarrassing situation. Hannah's expressions toward the unsuspecting stranger grew more hostile with

17

Chapter Two: *Heartfelt*

every affectionate gesture. When Rachel reached in the man's direction, arms outstretched, inviting the man to come pick her up, Hannah knew it was time to go. She whisked Rachel up out of her chair and told Tom she would be waiting in the car.

Hannah walked toward the door with Rachel in her arms. That is when she saw that the stranger was situated right in the pathway to the exit. Hannah was determined to walk by the stranger without a word, though if she could somehow display her displeasure, she certainly would. She not only felt threatened by the man, but now she was angry with him for ruining the night's festivities.

Just as Hannah reached the man's seat, Rachel leaped without warning from her mother's arms and into the waiting embrace of the foul-smelling stranger. Immediately they entered into a love fest, the man holding Rachel tightly to his shoulder and rocking her back and forth and the little girl cooing and laughing with delight.

As Hannah was reaching out to retrieve Rachel, she saw tears appear from under the man's heavy eyelids. She was paralyzed as the tenderness of the moment swept over her. Their embrace lasted only a moment before the man opened his swimming eyes and placed Rachel back into the arms of her anxious mother. With a weak, raspy voice he looked at Hannah and simply said, "Thank you, ma'am.

Thank you with all my heart. Most folks won't let me near their children. That one's a special little girl, ma'am. You take good care of her, OK?"

With those words, the man walked out the door and left Hannah standing stunned and silent. A few minutes later when Tom reached the car, he found Hannah with her face in her hands crying. "Hannah, what's the matter?" Tom asked.

"Oh Tom, God used my Rachel to teach me a hard but necessary lesson tonight. Every person alive deserves to be loved. Whether we are tattered or tailored, rich or poor, we all need to feel the warm embrace from someone who doesn't see our filthiness or our frailties. I saw God do that tonight through our little girl. The heartfelt thankfulness that stranger expressed will never leave me. Nor will the love that Rachel gave to him."

Now that you have **purified** yourselves

by obeying the truth

so that you have **sincere** love for your brothers,

love one another deeply,

from the heart.

1 Peter 1:22

Man may dismiss compassion from his heart, but God never will.

—William Cowper

Thankful

Heartfelt

Awesome

Natural

Kindness

You-nique

Optimistic

Unforgettable

CHAPTER 3

Awesome

Few things in life are truly awesome. Think about it: the word means "inspiring awe." Although it gets thrown around too casually in today's culture, once in a while it applies:

- ❋ a breathtaking sunset
- ❋ music so moving it makes you cry
- ❋ the rush of love at first sight
- ❋ that initial glimpse of your newborn baby
- ❋ a starry, starry night
- ❋ the kindness of a true friend

You are a true friend—and your kindness fills me with awe. For that, I thank you.

DEUTERONOMY 10:21

24

"He is your praise;

he is your God,

who performed for you those great

and awesome wonders you saw

with your own eyes."

Two things fill me with constantly increasing

admiration and awe,

the longer and more earnestly I reflect on them:

the starry heavens without

and the moral law within.

—Immanuel
Kant

The Dream

She pulled into town one cool, autumn afternoon, driving slowly down the main street. She stopped at the only traffic light before parking in front of the grocery store. Carolyn bought bread, bologna, cheese, pickles, chips, and a Coke. Then she climbed back into her car and drove to the edge of town, where she noticed a small park in a grove of elm trees. She stopped there to eat her picnic lunch.

As she dumped her trash into the metal barrel, Carolyn caught her breath. There it was! At long last, after her five-year search, she had found it. Tucked into a secluded spot in the woods stood a little deserted cottage—the one she had always imagined as her writing retreat. A dirt path led from the park to the cottage's front gate.

Walking slowly along the path, Carolyn tried to soak up every detail around the small, deserted building. Fallen elm leaves crunched beneath her feet as she walked reverently through the

Chapter Three: *Awesome*

white-picket gate and up the old brick walk to the front porch. She tried the front door, and it opened without resistance. A quick inspection made her heart beat a little faster with anticipation. It was the perfect place for a well-known author to find the anonymity and solitude necessary for writing.

Returning to the front porch, Carolyn sat down in the swing and began to push it gently back and forth, back and forth. Its metal chain squeaked softly in rhythm with her thoughts: *It needs new paint, and the shingles on the roof have to be replaced. The roses need to be pruned, and the lawn has to be mowed. But mostly, it needs someone to live in it, love it, care for it. It's perfect! I wonder why it's empty. Is it for sale?*

A sudden impulse sent Carolyn running back to her car. She drove quickly back into town and found the local real estate office. When she asked about the little cottage, she learned that it had been repossessed by the bank; its former owners couldn't pay the back taxes. All she had to do was pay the taxes, and it was hers…which is exactly what Carolyn did.

Handing her the key and deed to her new writing retreat, the real estate agent told her about a local fix-it man named Henry. He could help her make the needed repairs. Carolyn stopped to talk to him on her way back to the cottage and arranged for him to begin work the next day.

By mid-December all the repairs had been made. The roof no longer leaked, the cottage had a fresh coat of pale yellow paint and forest green shutters, the lawn had a manicured look, and Carolyn had added some homey touches inside. It was the perfect haven for writing. Soon she could sit down at her desk overlooking the goldfish pond and begin working on her next novel.

One chilly afternoon as Carolyn swept the leaves off the front porch, she heard a small voice say, "Hello." Looking up, she saw a little red-haired girl swinging on the front gate.

"Well, hello," said Carolyn with a smile. "What's your name?"

"Jenny. What's yours?"

"Carolyn."

"How do you like the house?" the little visitor asked.

"I love it. It's just what I've always wanted."

"We liked it too," said Jenny. "It looks nice with the new paint."

Carolyn stopped sweeping. "Thanks. Did you live here?"

"Yes, until my daddy died. Then we had to move."

"Where do you live now?" Carolyn asked with concern.

"In the shelter downtown."

Chapter Three: *Awesome*

Carolyn put down her broom and walked out to the gate. "I'm sorry your daddy died. What happened?"

"He was sick for a long time, and he couldn't work. The doctors couldn't make him well. They said he had something called leukemia. He died last year, just before Christmas. Then the bank told Mama that we'd have to move. She cried a lot after that."

"I'm so sorry, Jenny. Say, I've got some lemonade inside. Would you like some?"

"Thanks, but I have to go now. My mom will be worried about me. I have to take care of my baby brother while she cooks dinner at the shelter. Maybe I'll come back sometime."

"Please do," Carolyn said quietly as Jenny walked away, glancing back at the little cottage wistfully two or three times before she was out of sight.

Suddenly Carolyn's happy little cottage—her dream—seemed sad and lonely. In her mind she could see Jenny and her family playing in the yard. She could imagine the smell of homemade bread baking in the small kitchen. She could hear the sounds of laughter that now seemed to echo eerily in the trees. And she knew what she had to do.

On Christmas Eve, Henry, dressed up in a Santa Claus suit, rang the bell at the downtown shelter. He entered with a happy, "Ho Ho

Ho!" and started giving presents to all the children. He handed Jenny a special doll with red hair just like hers, and he had a big, blue rubber ball for Jenny's baby brother.

The last thing in Santa's sack was an ordinary white envelope. He walked quietly over to Jenny's mother and said, "Sarah, this is for you." Looking quizzically at him, Sarah took the envelope and tore open the sealed flap. When she removed a piece of paper from the envelope, a key fell into her lap. She recognized it immediately. When she looked at the paper, she realized it was the deed to the cottage—with her name on it—marked "Paid in Full."

Tears welled up in her eyes as she pulled out the second piece of paper. The light blue note read, "Please come home. I miss you. Merry Christmas." It was signed, "The Cottage by the Park."

"Who would do such a thing?" Sarah asked Henry, her soft eyes searching for answers.

"She told me I could never tell you who she is, but I can tell you this: She really wanted that little cottage for herself, but her big-hearted kindness wouldn't allow her to keep it when she learned about your situation."

"I just can't believe it. I can't believe someone would do this for me...for my children." Sarah's bewildered face showed the signs of a year's worth of worry and grief.

"Will you do something for me, Henry?" Sarah pleaded. "Will you tell her how much this means to me? Will you tell her that what she has done will change the lives of my children forever? Please tell her how thankful I am...please tell her *thank you*."

Come and see what God has done,

how awesome

his works in man's behalf!

Psalm 66:5

Gratitude bestows reverence,

allowing us to encounter everyday epiphanies,

those transcendent moments of awe

that change forever how we experience

life and the world.

—John Milton

Thankful
Heartfelt
Awesome
Natural
Kindness
You-nique
Optimistic
Unforgettable

CHAPTER 4

Natural

If I could order nature, I would ask the sun to shine on you today. I would request flowers in a rainbow of colors to bloom at your feet. The grass leading up to your door would always be a soft, green carpet—never in need of mowing—and the birds in the trees would call out your name.

Your friendship inspires the best in me! Kindness must be second nature to you. Thank you.

Praise the LORD from the earth,

you great sea creatures and all ocean depths,

lightning and hail, snow and clouds,

stormy winds that do his bidding,

you mountains and all hills,

fruit trees and all cedars,

wild animals and all cattle,

small creatures and flying birds.

Psalm 148:7–10

Beauty is the mark God sets on virtue.

Every natural action is graceful;

every heroic act is also decent,

and causes the place and the bystanders to shine.

—Ralph Waldo
Emerson

"My lilies need to be watered,"
The heavenly master said;
"Wherein shall I draw it for them,
And raise each drooping head?"

Close to His feet on the pathway,
Empty, and frail, and small,
An earthen vessel was lying,
Which seemed of no use at all.

But the Master saw, and raised it
From the dust in which it lay,
And smiled as He gently whispered:
"This shall do my work today.

"It is but an earthen vessel,
But it lay so close to me;
It is small, but it is empty,
And that is all it needs to be."

Anonymous

Creativity is a natural extension

of our enthusiasm.

—Earl Nightingale

Thankful

Heartfelt

Awesome

Natural

Kindness

You-nique

Optimistic

Unforgettable

CHAPTER 5

Kindness

Simple kindnesses, whether from strangers or longtime friends, make the world worth living in. Sometimes they catch us by surprise; other times we see them coming. However they drop into our lap, they are welcome visitors—little reminders that God and goodness still live in human hearts.

Your kindness to me did not go unnoticed.

COLOSSIANS 3:12

Therefore, as God's chosen people,

holy and dearly loved, clothe yourselves

with compassion, kindness, humility,

gentleness and patience.

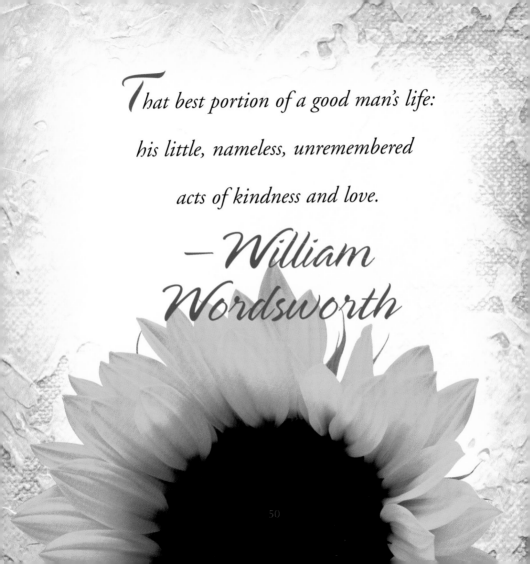

That best portion of a good man's life:

his little, nameless, unremembered

acts of kindness and love.

—William
Wordsworth

A Hidden Blessing

Shelby Seeger sat in the Memphis airport at gate A33 waiting for her flight to board. Gate A33 was the last one on the A concourse—a remote tentacle of the terminal reaching toward sparsely populated parts of the country. Shelby needed anonymity, and she thought a small town would provide the refuge she was seeking for the mission she was on. Her heavy heart felt the implications of her remote status, as if banished from the mainstream of life.

Three weeks earlier, Shelby's world had been turned inside out. When she discovered she was pregnant, her boyfriend had abandoned her, and her career plans had taken a sharp turn south. Shelby was an amateur model, unmarried, and now expecting an unwanted child. Though she had always been very close to her parents, particularly her father, she decided she would not tell them of her plight, knowing they would be hurt, ashamed, and embarrassed. *They have sacrificed so much to get me through college and help her get started in life. Why not spare them the pain of knowing this?* she had reasoned. She resolved to suffer alone because she had failed them in spite of all they had done for her.

The gate attendant announced the boarding protocol. As she approached the stairway leading down to the tarmac, Shelby's burdened heart betrayed her to an observant elderly gentleman with soft, white hair and a beard to match. He watched her diligently, however discreetly, as she climbed the narrow steps onto the small prop plane and found her seat next to a window in the back of the aircraft. Noting her heaviness of spirit, the elderly man knew he could not ignore her need for the sake of his own convenience.

He waited until everyone had boarded before asking the heavy-set, middle-aged woman next to Shelby if he could trade seats with her, pointing to an aisle seat several rows up. He explained that he needed to be in close proximity to the lavatory.

Though preoccupied with greater concerns, Shelby dreaded spending the next two hours sitting beside an elderly man with who-knows-what kind of infirmity. Her mind repulsed at the thought of an undisclosed illness, especially since she was feeling quite nauseated these days.

He smiled at her, adjusting his safety belt and settling into his seat. She smiled back, with reticence, hoping he caught on to the fact that she wasn't open to conversation. Reaching for her book, she shifted slightly toward the window, signaling that their interaction had reached its completion. Surely the old man would read her body language and leave it at that.

The minutes ticked by sluggishly. Tortured in her spirit, Shelby prayed for the pace to pick up. She wanted to get this over with as quickly as possible. The thought of going through an abortion alone frightened her, and her conscience was beginning to emerge from its numb darkness, seizing her heart with unexpected waves of emotion and erupting through her eyes in unannounced torrents of tears. She wished her dad were there beside her instead of this aged stranger. She had always relied on her dad to take care of her, but she couldn't turn to him now and risk breaking his heart. He had loved her so deeply and protected her from life's hard knocks. But now she must protect him.

The plane's first movement was snail-like, but it quickly picked up speed, lurching into the sky with an awkward and unmerciful surge of motion. Shelby's nauseous stomach reacted violently to the turbulent takeoff. Dropping her book, she grabbed for the bag in the seat pocket in front of her, a cold sweat washing over her face and sending a tremor through her body and out through her hands. Her trembling fingers fumbled the bag, and panic gripped her heart as she felt herself losing control of the situation.

Suddenly, one strong yet gentle hand grasped her around the shoulders and held her firmly as she heaved forward, while another took hold of the bag and held it unwaveringly to her mouth until her vomiting ceased.

In one graceful movement, the old man was out of his seat, tossing the bag into the lavatory, and back with his handkerchief in hand mopping Shelby's face with tenderness and compassion. Weak and exhausted, Shelby offered no resistance. She resigned herself to his gracious embrace for the moment with gratitude and relief borne of humiliation.

Within minutes, a flight attendant approached them, having noticed the activity, and remarked, "Well, young lady, you are fortunate to have your father traveling with you."

"More like grandfather," the old man responded with a lilt in his voice, looking at the flight attendant. "I am old enough to be her grandfather," he continued, turning back to Shelby, "and might add that I would be honored and thankful if I were. However, I am not, so my boasting ends with this: I have been blessed to know her only since boarding this plane."

Shelby hadn't looked at his eyes until then. Now that she saw them, she couldn't help but notice that they were deep, brown pools of compassion in which she saw herself swimming, completely immersed in a look of love and understanding.

Chapter Five: *Kindness*

"Thank you so much, sir," she stammered, riveted on his eyes. "I heard you say you were ill, and yet you ended up taking care of me. I'm so sorry for the inconvenience and discomfort I might have caused you, but don't worry, at least I'm not contagious."

"I'm not ill," he assured her smiling. "I'm a healthy old ox, but I've been around awhile and I know heartache when I see it. I thought you might need some support, so I was, in effect, volunteering for the job. You see, I have a granddaughter about your age, and I live in a state of expectant hope that if she ever needs help, there will be some trustworthy old soul who will be there for her in my absence."

"I'm not sick either," Shelby said. "I'm pregnant." Her eyes lowered as she labored to release those last words.

"Well, congratulations!" he responded, grinning broadly. "I'm relieved to know that it is a hidden blessing that has such a beautiful young woman in turmoil."

"Thanks," Shelby muttered heavily, intending to end the conversation at that. She straightened her sweater, smoothed her hair, and fished her book from between the seats, where she had dropped it. Her mind seized onto the words, *a hidden blessing*. She couldn't help consider the irony that it was shame she was hiding and there was no apparent blessing in this situation. Tears stung her eyes without warning, and she tried to blink them away. But one salty rebel broke through the barrier of her lashes and splashed with open treason onto the page of her book—publishing to her seatmate that the turmoil was not ended. She hoped in vain that he had not seen the tiny liquid traitor.

"Is your father living?" he queried.

"Yes, he is, and I wish he were here," she said sniffing, stifling a sob.

Wisdom spoke through the wrinkled lips of discernment: "I wish you could meet my granddaughter. She is a lot like you—dignified and poised. My dear child, your own father's heart will be so graced in his old age by the child that inhabits your womb. Have you told him yet?"

Shelby looked up incredulously. *Dignified and poised!* "Sir, I find it amazing that you would describe me in those words, when ever since you sat down beside me I have been completely out of control. The answer is no, I haven't told my father, nor do I intend to. It would break his heart, because I am not married."

The old man reached for her hand and squeezed it gently as he spoke: "A man's heart is built to absorb the pain of those he loves. It is his calling. Far greater would be his sorrow if he knew he hadn't been given the opportunity to be there for you when you needed him

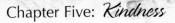

most, for his devotion to you has nothing whatsoever to do with your marital status," he whispered. "He loves you because you are his."

There was silence for several seconds. "I'm an old man; I know these things." He squeezed her hand a little tighter.

She ventured to look back into his warm eyes, searching for hope, for help.

"Would you do me a favor?" he asked.

"How could I say no after what just happened?" she responded. "I owe you, don't I?"

"No, my dear, you don't. We exist for this, to lend a hand in time of need. But when this plane lands, if you would call your father for me, I would be forever grateful." He winked and smiled, returning her hand to her lap.

Months later, in the spring of the year, Shelby Seeger gave birth to a beautiful baby girl. Holding the tiny wonder in his arms for the first time, Shelby's father spoke his heart and hers as he looked toward heaven and prayed: "Thank you, Lord, for this precious life, my granddaughter; and for the joy, the pain, and the privilege of loving. And thank you, Father, for providing my child, on that fateful flight headed for a world of hurt, the wisdom that turned her heart toward home."

We cannot tell the precise moment

when friendship is formed.

As in filling a vessel drop by drop,

there is at last a drop which makes it run over.

So in a series of kindness there is, at last,

one which makes the heart run over.

— *James Boswell*

Thankful

Heartfelt

Awesome

Natural

Kindness

You-nique

Optimistic

Unforgettable

CHAPTER 6

You-nique

There are some people who cross my path who do just that—cross my path. They leave no lasting impression in my mind. They blend together in a sea of faces in my memory. But then there are others like you who have left an indelible mark that can never be erased even with the passing of time.

Thank you for being "you-nique"—someone whom I will never forget, someone so easy to love. I will always remember you!

You made all the delicate,

inner parts of my body

and knit me together in my mother's womb.

Thank you for making me

so wonderfully complex!

Your workmanship is marvelous—

and how well I know it.

Psalm 139:13–14 NLT

65

Wishing to be friends is quick work,

but friendship is a slow-ripening fruit.

—Aristotle

I created you and have cared for you since before you were born. I will be your God throughout your lifetime—until your hair is white with age. I made you, and I will care for you. I will carry you along and save you.

Isaiah 46:3–4 NLT

You are God's workmanship,

a quilt of beauty to behold.

— Karla Dornacher

Thankful

Heartfelt

Awesome

Natural

Kindness

You-nique

Optimistic

Unforgettab

CHAPTER 7

Optimistic

Whenever I think of people who mean the most to me, your face always comes to mind. You may not realize it, but you're one of those rare individuals called "balcony people"—always optimistic, always cheering me on and shouting "You can do it!" from the top row.

For that I want to thank you.

Your optimism inspires me. Because I have you for a champion, I'm encouraged to help others as well. My prayer is that they, in turn, might give others a spiritual boost, creating a daisy chain of optimism that started with one special balcony person—you!

"For I know the plans I have for you,"

declares the LORD,

"plans to prosper you

and **not** to harm you,

plans to give you **hope**

and a future."

Jeremiah 29:11

Hope is definitely not the same thing

as optimism. It is not the conviction that

something will turn out well,

but the certainty that something makes sense,

regardless of how it turns out.

—Vaclav Havel

Hope is the thing with feathers
That perches in the soul,
And sings the tune without the words,
And never stops at all.

And sweetest in the gale is heard.
And sore must be the storm
That could abash the little bird
That kept so many warm.

I've heard it in the chillest land,
And on the strangest sea;
Yet, never, in extremity,
It asked a crumb of me.

Emily Dickinson

Optimism is the cheerful frame of mind

that enables a teakettle to sing,

though in hot water up to its nose.

—Anonymous

Thankful

Heartfelt

Awesome

Natural

Kindness

You-nique

Optimistic

Unforgettable

CHAPTER 8

Unforgettable

The people in our lives are like threads in a tapestry—some prominent and bright, others woven here and there in faint colors. The completed tapestry of a life is the sum of all those threads woven into place.

Because of you, my life will never be the same. You took the time, you made the effort, and I was the one fortunate enough to have such a "bright thread" in my tapestry. Thank you.

ECCLESIASTES 4:9–10

"Two are better than one,
because they have a good
return for their work:
If one falls down,
his friend can help him up."

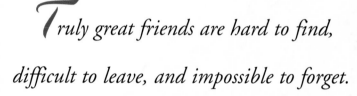

Truly great friends are hard to find,

difficult to leave, and impossible to forget.

—G. Randolf

A Forgiven Hero

Cameron had just moved into the small southern community of Ocean Springs and felt the full weight of loneliness. He was eight years old and in need of new friends. In his former neighborhood, he'd had many friendships and was considered one of the most popular kids in town. It was easy to see why. His face displayed fine features, topped by thick black hair, beautiful blue eyes, and a personality that could soften a porcupine. He was not a boy who was drawn to mischief or to kids who caused trouble. But being new in town, his identity was shaken, and he took hold of the first group of boys he came upon.

Within minutes, the rather rough group of boys were inviting Cameron to join their club. Although he had instinctive misgivings, Cameron's strong desire to belong overcame his good judgment, and he asked what he had to do to join. Charlie, the self-proclaimed leader of the group, took a step forward and looked straight into

Chapter Eight: *Unforgettable*

Cameron's eyes. Spitting arrogantly on the sidewalk, he looked at the other boys for assent, then spoke: "Well, if you want to be a part of the Panthers, you will have to go down this street to the gray and white house on the corner. That's old Miss Trumont's place. We all hate her because she is so mean. What you have to do is take a rock and throw it through her picture window. If you do that, you will be a full-fledged member of the Panthers. Now, what do you say?"

Cameron looked down for a few seconds, kicking at the dust. "I don't know about that. If you are so upset about her being mean, why do you want me to do something mean to her? That doesn't make sense."

Charlie quickly spoke up, "That's just what I thought, guys. Cameron is a wimp, and I'm afraid wimps don't mix well with Panthers."

He looked at Cameron again and mocked him in a squeaky voice, "There is a girls' group over on the next block called the Pink Carnations, and I am sure you would fit in great with them."

The needling worked. Cameron found himself picking up a large stone and stomping off toward Miss Trumont's house. The group, knowing they had gotten to him, marched off behind him, eager to see the action unfold.

The reputation Susan Trumont had with the boys mirrored the one she possessed with the rest of the community. She was in her mid-thirties, with a square build, black unmanaged hair, sunken eyes, and a notoriously short temper. She knew that no one cared about her; therefore, she was not going to look out for anyone else. The less she had to do with her neighbors, the better—and vice versa.

When the boys turned the corner, Susan just happened to be looking out of the window through which Cameron intended to hurl his stone. She noticed that he stood alone out in front of all the other boys. Suddenly, he reared back and gave the stone a whopping toss. The window shattered in a hundred pieces right in front of her. The noise was so loud that Cameron and the other boys stood in stunned silence. That is, until Miss Trumont appeared on the porch, running down the steps in hysterics.

"What in the world do you think you are doing, you bad boys?" she screamed at the top of her lungs.

The boys disappeared in a flash, except Cameron. When he heard her lump him with those "bad boys," he felt a sudden surge of sorrow for the broken window and simply stood there until she reached him.

"Do you realize what you have done, young man?" cried Susan.

Chapter Eight: *Unforgettable*

Cameron lowered his head and softly said, "Yes, and I am very sorry I did it."

"What is your name and where do you live?" Miss Trumont demanded.

"My name is Cameron Sims, and I just moved in about three blocks from here," he responded.

"Well, Cameron, you and I are going to pay a visit to your parents right this minute," she said.

"Yes ma'am," Cameron surrendered.

The knock on the door was answered by Cameron's mother. Her appearance was the exact opposite of Susan Trumont's. She was tall and lean with soft, brown hair. Her smile seemed a permanent fixture on her face.

After introducing herself, Susan started right in. "You have a problem child here, Mrs. Sims, and I want him kept away from me and my property. I also want you to pay for the picture window he broke today."

Cameron's mom looked at him, searching his eyes. He nodded his head in a confessional response. She then looked at Susan and explained that they had just arrived in town and the move had been hard on Cameron. "He is a very good boy, Miss Trumont, with a very good heart, and I am sure that nothing like this will ever happen again. You can be sure that Cameron will pay for the window—every penny."

Miss Trumont responded with a gruff, "I certainly hope so," then she turned and walked away with heavy steps.

Cameron knew his mother had an understanding heart, and her willingness to forgive him made the moral failure burn in Cameron's soul. He

Chapter Eight: *Unforgettable*

had to make it right. He prayed for a chance to make it up to Miss Trumont.

Two days later Cameron was walking down the street and encountered the same group of boys taunting Miss Trumont as she was walking home with an armload of groceries. The boys were unrelenting, especially Charlie.

Cameron stood on the sidewalk and stepped between Miss Trumont and the Panthers. "OK, guys," Cameron said, "this has gone far enough. Miss Trumont never did anything to any of you. From now on, if I catch any of you giving her trouble, you are going to have to answer to me."

Charlie stepped forward and spit. "Is that supposed to scare us?" he sneered.

"Not everyone, Charlie, just you. Because the first person I'll call on will be you. Is that understood?"

Charlie's face dropped, and he motioned the boys to walk away with him. Cameron quickly turned to a startled Susan Trumont. "Miss Trumont, I would like to help you carry those groceries home if you will let me. I know what I did was wrong, and I want to make it up to you."

A Forgiven Hero

That day Susan Trumont changed, not only toward Cameron, but toward the whole community. Everywhere she went, she told the story about her hero Cameron Sims and how he had become her protector and friend. She also admitted her wrong judgment of the boy. And although Miss Trumont thanked Cameron for that unforgettable day, Cameron was most thankful for the unforgettable forgiveness and confidence he received from his hero, his mother.

I will remember the deeds of the LORD;

yes, I will remember your miracles of long ago.

I will meditate on all your works

and consider all your mighty deeds.

Psalm 77:11–12